Ruth Olde.

Landscaping
MADE EASY BY DESIGN

Ruth Olde

PEANUT BUTTER PUBLISHING

Canadian Cataloguing in Publication Data

Olde, Ruth, 1952~
Landscaping made easy by design
ISBN 0-89716-826-7
1. Gardens—Design. 2. Landscape gardening. I. Title
SB472.45.O53 1999   712'.6   C99-900112-4

Edited by Neall Calvert
Design by Andrew Johnstone and Jason Kirby
Photographs by Ruth Olde

First Published 1999
Printed in Korea

PEANUT BUTTER PUBLISHING
Suite 212–1656 Duranleau Street • Granville Island
Vancouver, B.C. V6H 3S4
Telephone: (604) 688-0320

301–Pier 55 • 1101 Alaskan Way
Seattle, WA 98101-2982
Telephone: (206) 748-0345

TABLE OF CONTENTS

FOREWORD

Before I met Ruth I believed having a garden was like having an unwanted second job. You cut the grass. You bought the annuals. You planted the annuals at the edge of the grass. You watered the annuals. You cut the grass. And when the work was done you went inside.

"No, no, no!" said Ruth. "The point is to move outside into a room made for living."

She pushed back her hat and started walking around my square patch of grass, shaking her head. "This is like having a picture frame with nothing in it."

She is *the* outdoor architect and artist. Despite the mist and chill of that day she saw a rainbow for this postage stamp of a yard. "A pond there. And a path over there so you can wander under the trellis that should go…" she turned around and pointed, "…right there."

To Ruth a garden is not separate from the house. It is an extension of the house with its own atmosphere and design. You use the kitchen for cooking, the rec room for TV and the garden for feeling alive.

But of course the garden is alive, and that makes it so much different from the other rooms. It is not quite a member of the family, but it is always changing, giving and requiring care, which makes it almost part of the family.

I have been lucky enough to see many of her gardens, and she makes these rooms for living seem so natural and inviting, you hesitate to go back into the house. They have spots for privacy and areas for play, and curves and walls and vistas. All of that inside a city-sized lot.

It almost seems magical — how with some shrubs and rocks she makes you feel cozy in a large area, or makes a shoebox back yard that is surrounded by neighbouring walls seem like acreage.

The only thing she can't do with a patch of ground is leave you looking at it as something to avoid.

Mike McCardell

Mike McCardell
BCTV Reporter, Vancouver
Aspiring gardener

ABOUT THE AUTHOR

Ruth Olde was born in Winnipeg on a spring day and left on the doorstep of a kindly minister and his wife. She grew up in the back pews of a church, so you know everything she says is honest and true, especially when it comes to landscape design.

She raised six children while studying design and continued to raise them while creating gardens. She was still raising them when gardens she had designed began winning awards. Many of her designs include play areas for children and secluded places for adults, a combination that ensures sanity, which Ruth still has.

When her children were old enough to feed themselves, Ruth began volunteering for civic duty in their town of Maple Ridge, B.C. She served on at least one committee for each child, helped design the future growth of the city and also helped others set up their own small businesses.

She and her life partner Gunther Blasig run Blasig Landscape Design and Construction Ltd.

in Maple Ridge, located 40 km (25 miles) east of Vancouver in the scenic Fraser Valley. Her employees are ordered to think of her as a kind and understanding boss.

On the speaking circuit, attendees use words such as *excellent, informed, provocative* and *humorous* to describe her lively presentations.

To the Reader:

This book is for anyone who has pored over garden magazines, dreaming of a garden, but not knowing where to start.

Planning is essential. After reading this, you should be able to organize your dreams and wishes and create a blueprint for your successful outdoor rooms. You can stage its development over whatever period you wish, knowing what the finished product will look like.

Good luck,

Ruth Olde

ACKNOWLEDGMENTS

The following people deserve special thanks: Jarrod McAleese and Reinier van de Poll for their landscape graphics and design contributions, Gunther Blasig and Alison Heaven for their patience and for keeping things running smoothly while I hid behind the screen to write this book. I also need to thank Mike McCardell for helping me bring my words to life, Jo Blackmore at Peanut Butter Publishing for keeping everything on track — and all our amazing clients, who are the reasons this book exists.

P.S. — Thanks especially to my children, who had the intelligence and grace to grow up and leave home—so I could create this book in peace and quiet.

[Carol's dilemma: a difficult slope, too much lawn, a bare fence — in short, too much work for too little pleasure]

WHY PLAN?

Carol's Story

The voice on the other end of the telephone said, "My name is Carol. Can I have anything I want in my garden?"

"Of course," was my immediate, sincere reply.

"Anything?"

"Of course," I added without hesitation.

"Several landscape designers have told me I couldn't."

By now, fear about what she actually did want was beginning to seize my thoughts, so it was time to ask — "What exactly do you want?"

"Oh, a British telephone booth, a Victorian gazebo, a few arbours, different level patios, a brickwalled compost area, gas lights, gas heaters." Carol paused.

"Is that all?" I asked.

"No, I want lots of annual beds, a birdbath, a pond and I think there are a few things that just won't come to mind right now."

"Is it a large property?"

"Well, it's an average city back yard, maybe a little smaller. Actually, it's quite narrow."

Contrary to what you may think, it didn't sound much more difficult than most gardens. Big dreams can fit into small spaces, and the best tool to make them work is a design.

When you build a house, you need a detailed construction plan so you will get what you want, and not waste time and money. Outdoor rooms are the same.

A design is economical. You can take as long as you need to fulfill it, and you will always know what your finished garden will look like. The logical progression of construction becomes obvious on a design. Even if you would like your hot tub first, it may not make sense to install it and then move it when you put in the patio. Generally speaking, hard materials (retaining walls, patios, decks, swimming pools, etc.) are the first step. Later, they can be protected when the topsoil or other construction materials are dragged across them to complete another stage.

Building materials, plants and long-term care can be expensive. A well-developed landscape plan, drawn to scale, takes the guesswork out of construction. You will be able to accurately assess the required quantities (square feet, lineal feet, lawn area, plant materials, etc.). If you are getting estimates on all or part of the work, you will sleep better knowing that all the estimates are on the same finished product, not on the best description you could give about what you want. Implementation can take years. But with proper planning, each stage can be enjoyed with a sense of accomplishment, and the assurance that it will all fit together in the end.

[The problem (left) — The yard needed a facelift to add colour and "rooms" to use at different times]

[The solution (below) — A design that combines various shapes, stretches the eye and provides "rooms" throughout the garden]

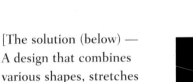

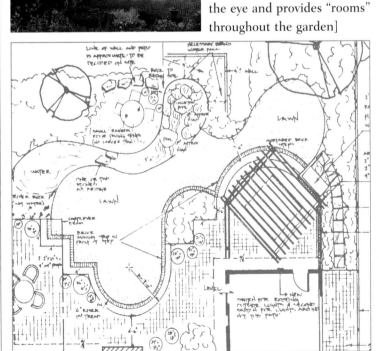

[The result (above) — A yard becomes a garden in which glass-covered areas provide protection and open areas encourage sun]

A design will place the right plants in the right place. They will flourish and not sprawl over their neighbours, or leave gaps that Mother Nature will fill with ugly, unmanageable weeds.

With a design, you can allow for different colours throughout the year and a variety of vistas to contemplate when you are forced to spend time inside. With a design, you can plan a virtually weed-free garden. Imagine a room that requires little cleaning. That alone should make the exercise worthwhile.

The question, then, is not whether you can afford a landscape plan, but whether you can afford to start without one.

So we drew Carol a plan. We kept changing it till it fit her vision and fulfilled her dreams. She got her red British phone booth — complete with a phone she could call England from. She got her gazebo, arbours…in short, everything on her list, and all the things she thought she had forgotten — all according to plan.

[Carol has everything she asked for — a symphony of colour and rooms galore]

Why a Professional Plan?

Now we come to the question you ask with your hands on your hips and your fingers just touching the top of your wallet. "Why should I pay someone to tell me what to do? After all, it's just a garden — I can do it myself."

That is true. I have a good friend who believes it, and every year he starts out with some rocks and seeds and bulbs and a head full of images and good intentions. And every year, he winds up with clumps of bushes that crowd out flowers, and the same straight pathway leading to them and a design that even he admits is locked somewhere between boring and embarrassing. And next year he will probably do the same, while insisting it's just a garden and he can do it himself.

Remember, a house built without a design might be interesting, but it's a poor bet as to whether it would be livable. A garden is your outdoor home; if it is well-designed, you will have the feeling that it is usable and sensible, and that you belong there.

When you hire a designer, you are purchasing services that are part technical and part artistic, and her or his fees will vary with experience and reputation. Ask around. Look for the type of gardens that you like, then find out who designed them. Interview several designers, as styles and personalities will vary, and you want to be sure it's a good match.

Once you have chosen a designer, the process should go something like this:

On-site consultation — a discussion of your garden's potential. A few hours with a professional should accomplish quite a bit. Upon completion, you should have a definite idea of where you are headed and what to do next. You should know what materials would be most appropriate for your site and your budget, and rough locations of living spaces and planting areas. Your thoughts on how to attain the privacy you long for — in fact, every whim of your imagination or desire that can be put into words — are up for discussion. That's part of what you pay a designer for.

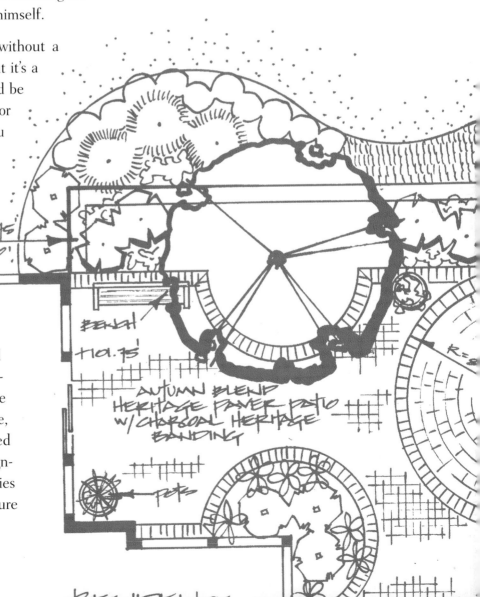

One visit may be enough, or it may take several consultations throughout the process to keep you on track. Design services can be tailor-made to your needs.

Landscape Design — a "map" of what your garden can become. Just like a map, it will be to scale and can be followed exactly to get where you want to go. A designer should be able to tell you what a plan will cost before you begin, with some contingencies for major changes. It is a two-step process. First the spaces are defined (patios, walkways, lawn, planting beds, retaining walls, etc.). Once these are approved, specific plants can be designated to fill the allotted areas. The construction phase often takes quite a while to complete, and changes can occur as the universe unfolds, so the

planting plan can be deferred until all the building is done. This defers cost, and is one less thing to worry about. Besides, ideas of how your garden will look evolve as you see things taking shape, so there is no rush to decide everything at the beginning of the process.

Construction. Whether your designer is part of a construction company or not, she or he should be able to assist during this stage as well. It may be something as simple as helping review estimates or suggesting companies that are reliable and capable, or the designer may offer an estimate of their own. The designer could also act as the project consultant, or simply make a few visits to the site to assure that the design is being followed. The goal is to ensure the success of the project and reduce your stress.

It should work like this: The designer will be solving problems while you watch your garden unfold. That is what you are paying for. At the end, you get to sit back and say, "This is just the way I dreamed it would be."

LAWN

TW +19.75
BW +100.0

ARBOUR
-SEE
DETAIL
SHEET 2.

GREY
ROMAN PAVER
WALK

LET'S GET STARTED

The term "landscape design" should apply to any outdoor area you are planning to change. No matter where it's located, or what size it is, it should be drawn out to scale.

For a planting bed: Drawing to scale allows proper spacing for plants. They will have enough space to flourish in their chosen manner, without interruption.

For an addition to a deck: Figuring out where the supporting beams will go, and how to wrap the deck around a corner, is far easier on paper than when your friends are standing around, anticipating pizza and beer, impatient to begin.

If you have a form survey, it will show the house foundations in relation to the property lines, and that is crucial. Perfectly square or rectangular lots are easy to draw, but others can be a nightmare to draw after the fact. Do not assume that the property line shown in the front of the house is the street — measure it. Measure everything. It doesn't cost any more. There are almost always several feet from the actual street or sidewalk to the property line. Many a design has been ripped up when this truth is discovered.

Use the house, unless it's going to be moved, as the reference point, and measure everything from there at right angles.

[How to measure property]

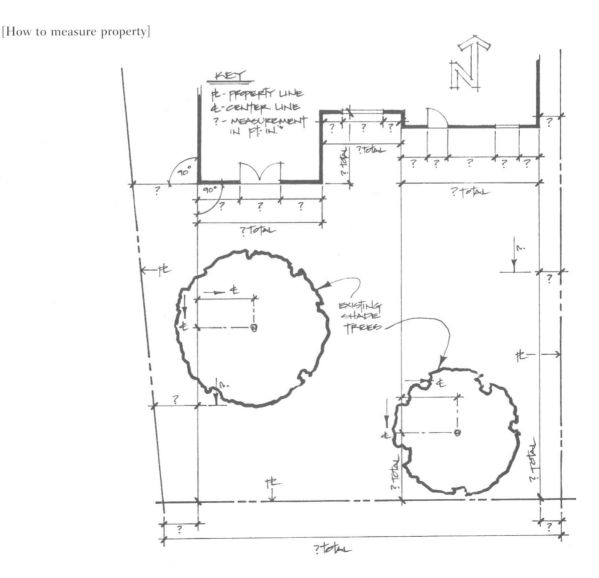

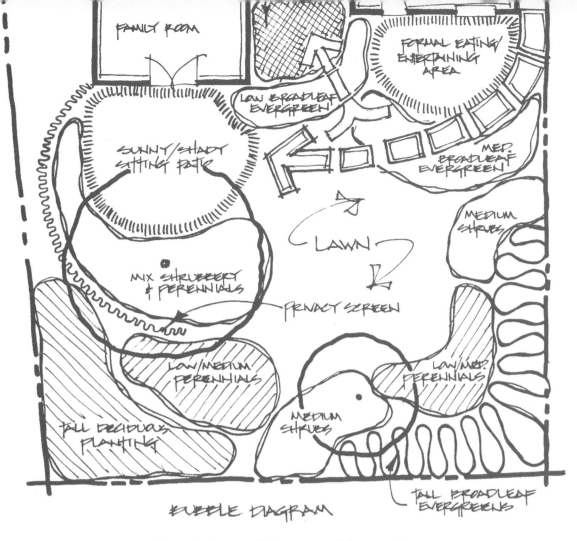

Labels in diagram: FAMILY ROOM · FORMAL EATING/ENTERTAINING AREA · LOW BROADLEAF EVERGREEN · SUNNY/SHADY SITTING PATIO · MED. BROADLEAF EVERGREEN · MEDIUM SHRUBS · MIX SHRUBBERY & PERENNIALS · LAWN · PRIVACY SCREEN · LOW/MEDIUM PERENNIALS · LOW/MED. PERENNIALS · TALL DECIDUOUS PLANTING · MEDIUM SHRUBS · TALL BROADLEAF EVERGREENS · BUBBLE DIAGRAM

[Roughly lay out all the pieces of the puzzle]

Locate existing features — hydro/telephone poles or boxes, trees, house vents, pathways, windows, and other landscape features that will be left as is.

Plans should be easy to read. Just pretend you are a bird surveying your property — not as a target, but as a picture about to be redrawn. All the lines are to scale, and represent an actual measurement on the ground. It's much easier with flat areas, but slopes will be indicated, even though they look flat on the page. If a retaining wall is shown, the height noted on the plan is always the height above ground. When calculating materials, the amount of the wall that needs to be buried for stability is extra.

It has been my experience that a plan always looks bigger on paper than when you are standing outside looking at it. Don't be deceived. If you've drawn it out properly, the plan will be exactly as you measured it.

Make a list of the things you want. Take your time. Simplify it by breaking it down into front and back. Visualize your ideal garden. You may be quite certain you don't have any ideas, but every thought may trigger an image of your dream garden. Spare no expense in the designing process. Budget can be considered later and, if necessary, some items eliminated then.

I recommend that you avoid making any major changes until you have lived with the property through at least four seasons. You will then know where you like to live outside. You will know where privacy is the most essential, where you need shade, or more sun. You will know where the traffic flows or doesn't flow, where you have a pond you didn't know about in August, and many other details not even considered yet.

But patience is a virtue seldom called upon when we want to make our new homes "ours" and perfect. I still want you to wait for those four seasons to pass, but in the meantime, I offer several options:

- Consult a professional. She or he should be able to assess and anticipate the potential problems that will become apparent as time passes — and get on with the design right away.

- Or — invest some money in pots that won't crack in the winter, and spread them around the property. Cluster them in groupings on the patio, by the front door, by the end of the sidewalk. Be sure that they are big enough and heavy enough that they won't disappear overnight. Change the plantings to match the seasons, and you will have excitement and interest while you plan other, more dramatic, changes.

If you have a new house, but no energy or budget left, level the ground, clean out the rocks and sticks, and plant grass. It is nature's way of getting rid of mud and it will carry you through until you have the finances and ideas that will make the garden your world.

It may be a long-term project, but it's the *planning,* not the budget or the size of the project, that counts.

Be constructive while you are waiting. Pay attention to the gardens in your neighbourhood and on the side roads on the way to and from work. Discover what you like and don't like as the year passes. Capture garden scenes with your camera. It's amazing how difficult it is to remember how something looked — or where it was — 20 minutes after you get home. Visit show gardens and write down the names of plants you love, the conditions they are growing in (e.g., full sun, wet ground, etc.) and how big they are. Even if you don't remember what they look like, you will know you liked them and you'll know if you can give them the same type of home.

You'll be so busy, that year will be gone before you know it!

Marriages can suffer ill effects over what goes where in the landscape. Discussing it all on a piece of paper is cheaper, easier and less public than arguing in the back yard. Or ask a landscape professional for help. Taking the above concerns into account, a designer's knowledge and experience will give life to your wish list — and you can disagree with them instead of each other.

List in hand and dreams in mind, make a bubble drawing (see page 7) of the desired areas. Except for the existing ones, don't think of plants right now. They are the icing on the cake, and you're not nearly ready for them yet.

HOLD ON — A QUIZ

Before you put pencil to paper, ask yourself the following:

1. Where does the sun get up, where does it set, and what does it do in between during the different seasons? How low is the sun in the winter?

   Gardens that people can live in have many demands made on them — lounging areas for sun worshippers, and arbours for red-heads to hide under.

2. Are there areas that are always very wet, or very dry?

   They can be used to advantage — a pond, a desert rockery — but cannot be ignored.

3. Is the property sloped?

   Slopes can appear much larger or smaller than they really are. Rent a builder's level and find out exactly what the slope is.

   Retaining walls may be necessary and can create perfect divisions between outdoor rooms. Knowing how high they will have to be before deciding where they will go makes the process faster and easier.

4. Is there a view you can steal, or one you would like to eliminate?

   Your landscape is not just what you pay taxes on. Look around. A well-thought-out wall can frame a view like a painting. A poorly planned one might cut it out entirely.

5. Where does the traffic flow all on its own?

   Changing the path of least resistance is one of the hardest battles to win. Try to put "hall-ways" where people will walk anyway.

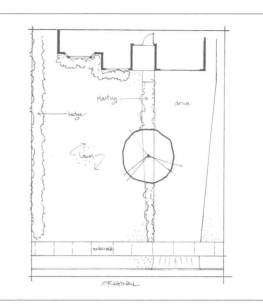

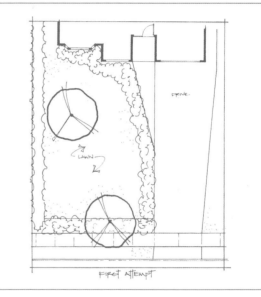

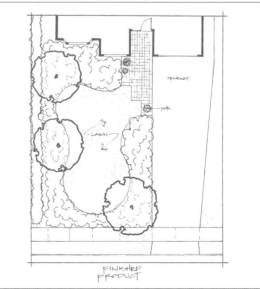

[Three stages of a design]

6. Are steps required?

Determine exactly how many, and how high they have to be, or they will haunt you later.

7. What type of soil do you have? Can you dig into it?

Building up on the existing terrain instead of battling with solid clay or rock might save countless hours and dollars. It might also extend your life span, and that of your marriage.

8. Which rooms do you want the most? How big must they be for you to enjoy using them?

One big, comfortable room is always better than two "I feel trapped, how do I get out of here?" rooms. Think BIG.

Hard surfaces may cost more to create, but installed properly they require less maintenance than planting beds or lawn. So don't be afraid to add square feet of hard surface. Create enough seating space for you, your family and friends, to sit uninterrupted while people move comfortably around you. Add some extra space for that beautiful pot, planter or bench you haven't seen yet, but will surely bring home. You'll be surprised at how much space you really need, and delighted with the results of your efforts.

Now start drawing —
> **change it —**
> **start again —**
> **change it —**
> **walk away in disgust —**
> **try again —**
> **tear out small portions of hair —**
> **try again.**

Don't give up.
This is the professional way.

A GARDEN OF ROOMS

By now, you will have either a rough sketch in front of you, or a whole pile of confusion. The confusion is frustrating, but not unusual. The garden of your dreams can be obstinate and difficult to fit into the space you pay taxes on.

So, let's break it down into rooms. Just like inside. That's really what you're creating, isn't it?

Would you ever say no to more closets?

Wouldn't it be convenient to have hallways instead of trampling the lawn or traumatizing the plants?

A nap in the hammock in the shady living room is as delicious as sneaking chocolate. Food cooked in outdoor kitchens has a special flavour.

Food shared in outdoor dining rooms makes summer memories.

Cozy corners for curling up in to enjoy the first or last rays of sunshine, are like window seats. They wrap us up and let us dream.

Be sure these rooms fit your wants and needs, and are in proportion to the space you have. A well-planned garden is a very personal, site-specific thing. Do not compromise for the sake of what should be included. Says who? It's your garden.

All rooms need some framework. Add walls, ceilings and floors for shade, privacy and convenience. They can be as open or as solid as you see fit. You can decorate them later with the perfect plants. Be sure you can enjoy these rooms from inside as well. There is much of the year you'll only be looking out at them.

And then begin — one room at a time.

[Garden view from inside — raised planter protects sunbathers at the pool from visitors' eyes]

WHICH ROOM GOES WHERE?

It's entirely up to you. Really, that's the beauty of it. As long as you'll use it wherever you put it. And generally, the following considerations guarantee that you will.

Sun-seeking

We are generally a rather lazy species. Any patio or deck intended to be used for lounging or eating is best located close to the house. But often they are in shade when we are most likely to use them. Don't despair. Look around.

You've already studied where the sun goes and when. And you know that while you can protect your body from its harmful rays, at certain times of the day or year, unless you are in the sun, you won't be sitting outside. You also know that, for some reason, most patios are shaded, cold and damp when you need the sun.

Sometimes just pushing the deck or patio beyond the corner of the house (see drawings this page) will add more sunny time and significantly increase the enjoyment of that room. Perhaps covering all or part of it from inclement weather will increase your enjoyment even more. A glass roof will serve as protection without darkening the inside rooms. A gas heater and lights add even more usable time. Before you know it, you'll only be going inside to use the bathroom.

If moving beyond the corner of the house creates a spot that is not private enough or too small to use, take another look around. There is always a spot that attracts the sun at different times than the patio. That will give you a reason to go out of your way to use it. Nestle it into its surroundings, and it will be a pleasure to use or look at year-round.

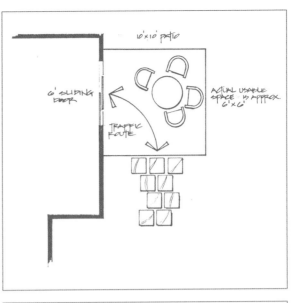

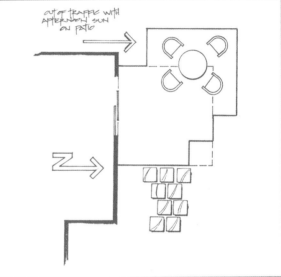

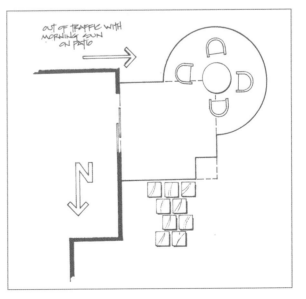

[Design a deck that peeks around the corner to find the sun]

Privacy

Mary said, "You have to create privacy, or I'll have to move. I just can't stand being outside with everyone watching us."

Conrad said, "No one is watching us. I don't want a hedge or a bunch of big trees making this yard small and dark."

Often the sole purpose of landscaping is to create a private haven. You should never apologize for that. Some sense of enclosure, separateness, peace and serenity provides a necessary release from everyday chaos and stress. This makes outdoor living rooms successful.

But be careful how you do it. Complete enclosure is difficult to achieve without putting a roof over your entire garden. Think about where you are the most comfortable. That's the spot to establish protection from well-intentioned neighbours hanging over the fence or the side of their balcony to chat. Concentrate on interrupting their line of vision.

[Glass protects outside rooms from the weather without shading inside rooms]

13

[At the end of the day when your outdoor dining room is in shade,
the arbour between the garage and house creates a sun-filled sitting room]

[The problem — Shaded in the
morning, scorching in the afternoon.
More shade in the afternoon, privacy
and living space was called for]

[The solution — The arbour, not
attached to the house, provides
shade and privacy, and a wonderful
sense of comfort and enclosure]

A tall hedge might do the trick. While a 6' fence is usually the maximum municipal regulations allow, we can have a 50' hedge if we desire. But who would? A hedge requires ongoing, often expensive maintenance, and can create shade and an undesirable micro-climate in your own garden. Maybe a partial hedge in a very specific spot, kept at an easily maintained height, would provide the desired effect.

[This cosy corner also provides a delightful view from the house all year round]

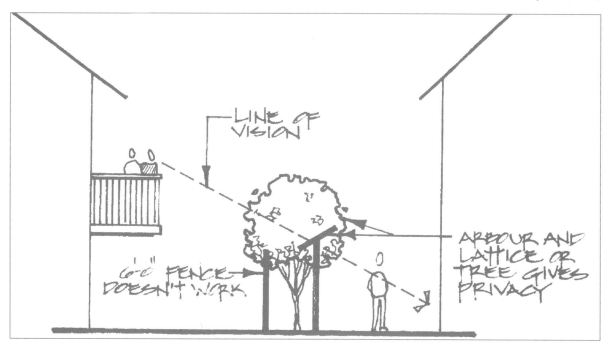

LINE OF VISION

6'-0" FENCE DOESN'T WORK

ARBOUR AND LATTICE OR TREE GIVES PRIVACY

[An open and airy screen still provides privacy]

Don't get me wrong. There are many beautiful, massive hedges doing a fabulous job of hiding private gardens from the street and from neighbours. I wish them no harm. I am referring to alternatives if you are starting from scratch, or have a space too small to consider such a solution.

An arbour might work. But be careful that it doesn't overly shade the patio or darken indoor rooms. The sun we avoid in the summer provides the light we cherish on dull winter days.

Consider one or more small (15'-20') deciduous trees whose canopy will protect in summer and whose leafless frame will let in light in winter. Remember that the height required for privacy when we are seated is different than that required when we are standing up or moving around.

I would never sacrifice light on a patio or deck to gain privacy. In my experience, shade or some sense of enclosure are almost always possible. But the path of the sun is, to date, beyond our control.

Mary now has a quiet, secluded reading spot under the grape arbour, and Conrad basks in the sun on his deck chair. One garden, two solitudes.

[There's nothing worse than wet shoes that get wetter left outside the door. An opaque roof allows inside rooms to remain light and boots to stay dry]

[Anyone home? Seclusion with a peek-a-boo wall]

[Simple lattice screening provides privacy and can include a window to the garden beyond]

Slip Sliding Away

Mark and Katherine live on a slope, actually the side of a mountain. They live there for the view of the ocean. After many years they tore down the little old house and built their dream home. Now it was time to build a garden.

Guessing the slope of a property can be as difficult as guessing how much rain actually fell after the sun comes out and the ground has absorbed it all. But it is crucial to the success of your design, so don't guess — figure it out accurately using a builder's level. You're only allowed a ½"-1" margin of error over the whole slope.

Slope is also relative. Deciding on whether to raise the patio to the floor level of the house — a step or two off the ground — is a far cry from desperately considering getting a goat to trim the grass on an unmanageable bank. And sometimes a slope is better left alone. If it hasn't slipped in the past few years, and whatever covers it requires little or no maintenance, it isn't broken — why fix it?

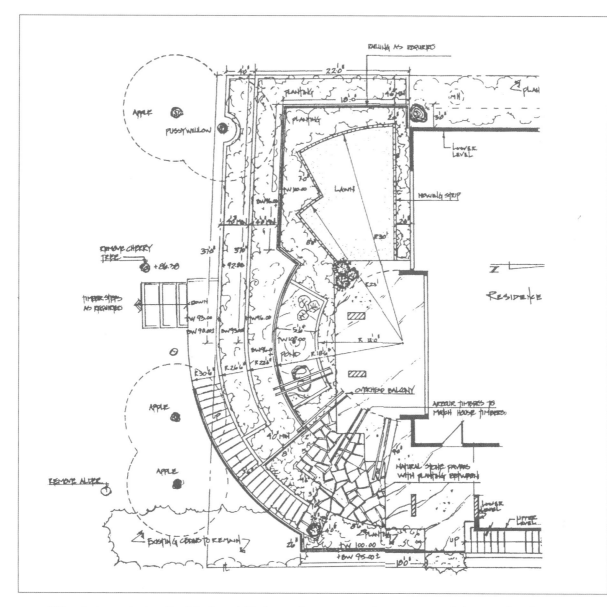

[The design solution for Mark and Katherine's mountain slope prevented their garden furniture from rolling downhill. Minimum use of retaining walls created maximum outdoor living room]

Slopes and responses to them are also very site-specific. I can accept no responsibility for ideas here that don't work on your particular slope. However, I am quite confident of the following:

- *As with all design decisions, maintenance is a key factor. Spending what can amount to considerable dollars on retaining walls is often made more palatable by the prospect of saving miserable, backbreaking hours weeding or mowing a steep slope.*

- *Walls higher than 4' need to be engineered. Check with your municipality, as allowable height and distance between retaining walls differ. The area between the walls need not be completely flat, but flatter usually equates to easier maintenance.*

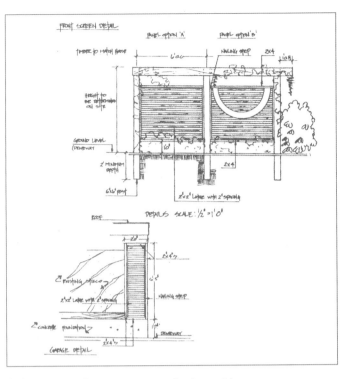

[The screen obscures cars parked outside Mark and Katherine's kitchen window]

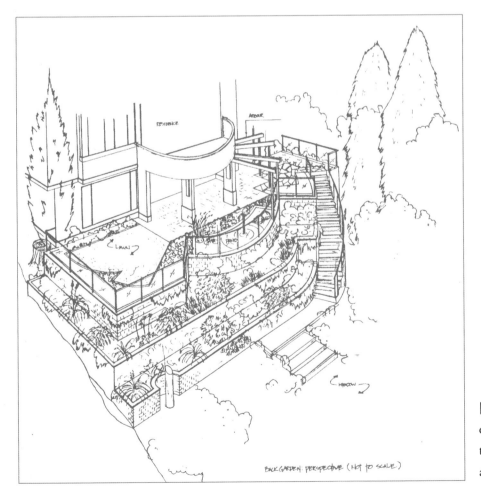

BACK GARDEN: PERSPECTIVE (NOT TO SCALE.)

[This perspective drawing allowed them to see how it all fits together]

[The problem — Instead of the Italian hillside villa they dreamed of, Jacqueline and Michael had a narrow trail zigzagging up a treacherous slope. It was difficult to maintain and even more difficult to negotiate]

- *Here are a few of your wall choices:*

  - ▸ dry stacked boulder
  - ▸ flat rock, dry or mortared
  - ▸ broken concrete
  - ▸ exposed aggregate
  - ▸ brick
  - ▸ wood
  - ▸ stacking concrete in a variety of shapes
  - ▸ smooth, stamped, stucco-faced or sculptured concrete

Each has a unique construction technique and appearance with varying degrees of cost and/or labour required. Its your choice, beauty is in the eye of the beholder.

- *Walls can be contoured. Not for the sake of making them more difficult to construct, but to make them less imposing and to visually add depth to a space already made narrower by their presence.*

[The solution — Hallways, walls and rooms galore, providing easy access, easy care and easy living]

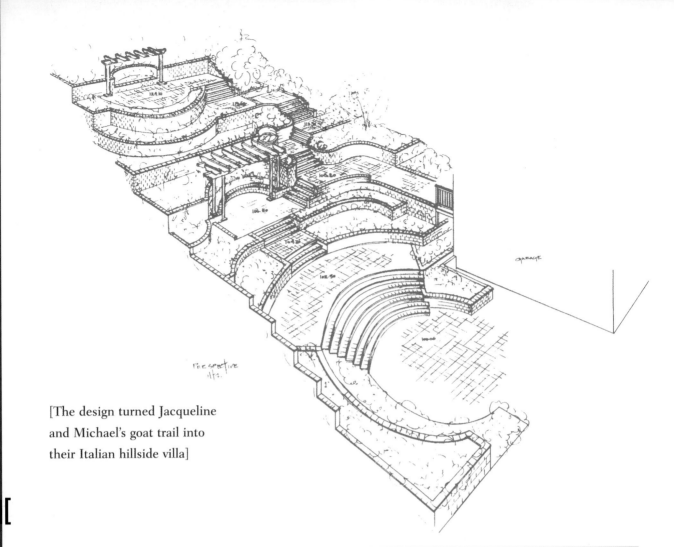

[The design turned Jacqueline
and Michael's goat trail into
their Italian hillside villa]

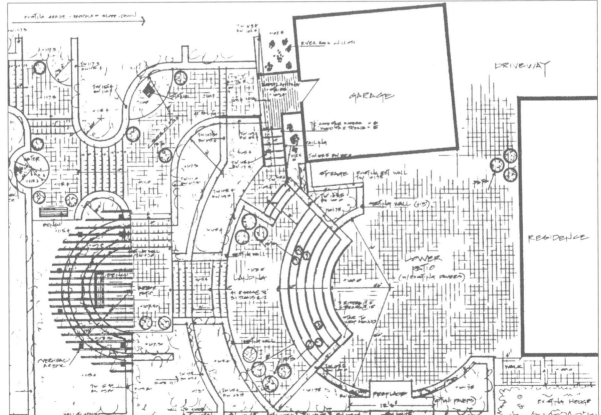

[Before]

[After]

[A planted wall on top of rock on filter cloth offers a solution for this hard-to-care-for slope]

[Using existing boulders to retain a significant slope cuts costs and fits in with original environment]

- *Build the first wall as far away from your living space as is physically or financially possible. That will maximize your usable space, especially when the slope is away from you and anything beyond that first wall visually disappears. The good news is that any lack of maintenance on your part won't be as noticeable, at least from your yard. The bad news is that you own it all, so you might as well use all you can.*

[Maximize usable space with a higher wall. An open wood wall assists drainage and feels less solid and imposing]

[Low walls can separate rooms without making the space in front of them seem smaller]

- Areas beyond the first wall may capture a view not available anywhere else in the garden and can be wonderful opportunities for a hidden retreat. But you need a darn good reason to go there, or they will be ignored.

- Walls at the edge of a patio area that are 16"-18" high with a wide cap (min. 12") can act as additional seats for guests. With or without cushions on special occasions, they will save money on furniture and delight adults and children alike.

- The first wall — the bottom wall — should be the same height or higher than the upper ones. Even the most well-built walls will appear to lean forward if the upper ones are higher than the lower ones. It's an optical illusion that can be quite disconcerting.

- Steps go hand in hand with walls. Whenever possible, it is best to build the walls that enclose the steps slightly higher than the risers. It makes you feel steadier when you go up or down, and the steps appear to come out of the ground, rather than being plunked on top of it. Every riser in a run of steps must be exactly the same height — no matter what. The rule is 2X the Riser + the Tread = 27". The ideal com-

bination is a riser of 6" and a tread of 15", but you can go to a minimum riser of 5" and a maximum riser of 7½" if necessary. There is a lot more room outside — don't be afraid to use it.

[Short, wide steps double as sitting benches during big parties, or any time for children, and are easy on the eyes and legs]

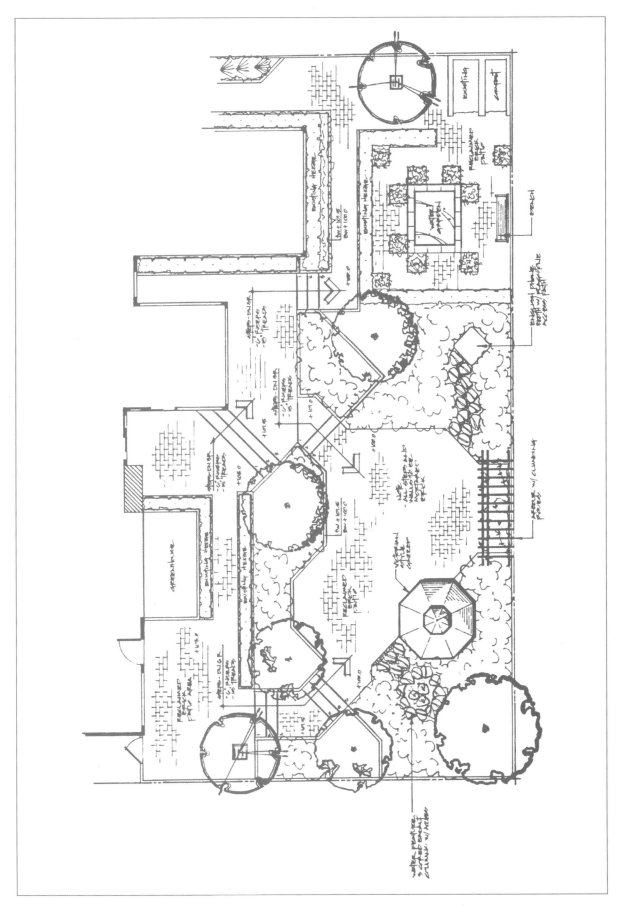

[Carol's design divided her garden into distinct rooms for sitting, entertaining and eating.
It included a gazebo for shelter and a water garden for tranquillity]

[The problem — A white wall that was blinding in the sun plus unevenly matched slopes made the entry unattractive and dangerous]

[The solution — A darkened wall, latticework, and stairs that turn into the courtyard make the entry inviting and cosy]

Remember Mark and Katherine's dilemma? Now they can walk out their back door onto a level patio with a pond, and climb down the stairs to their orchard. The retaining walls have created several gardens on the way to the ocean (see photos right and below).

It's still a beautiful view, it's just come closer.

[Above (before), left and below (after) — A reflecting pond behind the retaining wall draws in the distant view — and creates one to enjoy up close, too]

FRONT ROOMS

The first impression most people get of your home, of where you live, is gained not when they ring the doorbell, but when they park their car or walk by out front.

So let's make that impression a good one. Let's create an entry — a doorway — right there. An arbour or gate clearly establishes a street door. Add a fence, a formal hedge, or a variety of colourful shrubs, and you have a wall to support the doorway. Make the doorway wide; it will be an invitation to enter.

While your front garden adds to the flavour and character of your neighbourhood, it need not necessarily be completely open to everyone's view. Create a delineation between what belongs to you and what belongs to the street. A small wall, to retain a slight slope, or simply for effect, creates a strong boundary and defines a room. A fence will accomplish the same thing. The view into this front room can be completely blocked, or merely obscured slightly, creating a sense of mystery. Unfortunately security has to be kept in mind, so unless there is a gate that can be locked, a more open view may be appropriate.

Building walls or fences beyond the property line, which can be several feet back from the street, is not recommended. But that space can help set the tone for your garden entry. If there is no sidewalk at the street, a 2' wide paving-stone or stepping-stone path along the edge of the street allows people to get in and out of their cars without getting their feet wet or trampling your lawn or plants. At the street, flare the pathway to at least 6' or 8'. It will be your welcome mat.

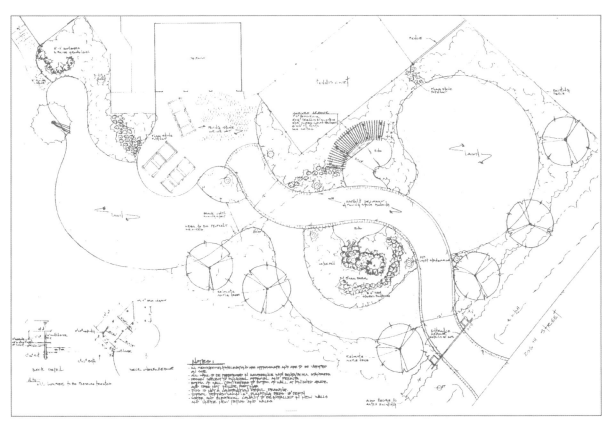

[Make the journey from the street to the house one that will add pleasure to your day.
Include features that will attract the eye and calm jangled nerves]

[The first impression any-one gets of your home is created when they stop their car out front, or stroll by. The welcome mat can be extended by creating a "front door" closer to the street. Paradoxically, such a door also extends your sense of privacy and enclosure]

A gently meandering path on the way to the door of the house lets people relax and unwind. Consider water. Size does not matter — the sight or sound of water is irresistible.

Rocks placed as sculptures, or lights, or actual figures along the path, will spark your visitors' imaginations, and the colour and texture of varied plants will delight their senses.

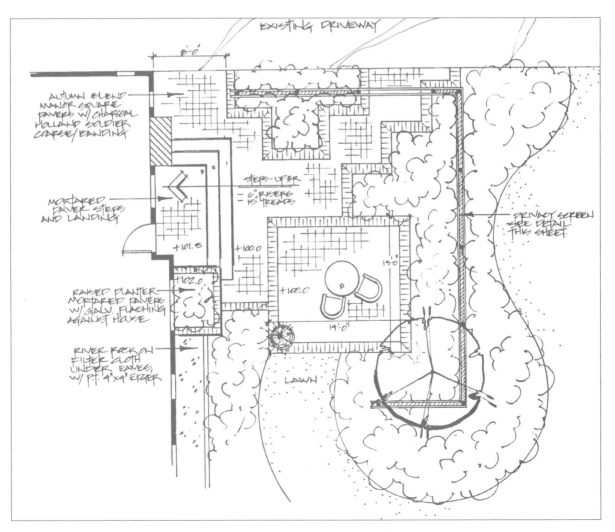

[A front-garden breakfast nook]

[Why not create a
room outside the front
door, hidden from the
entryway? Ben and
Laura asked...]

[...where they could
sit, sun and relax
beside the waterfall]

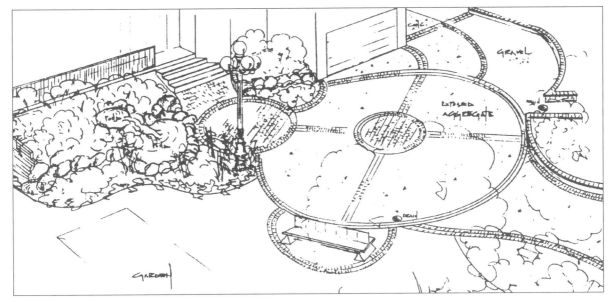

[Ben and Laura's front door...the original concept...]

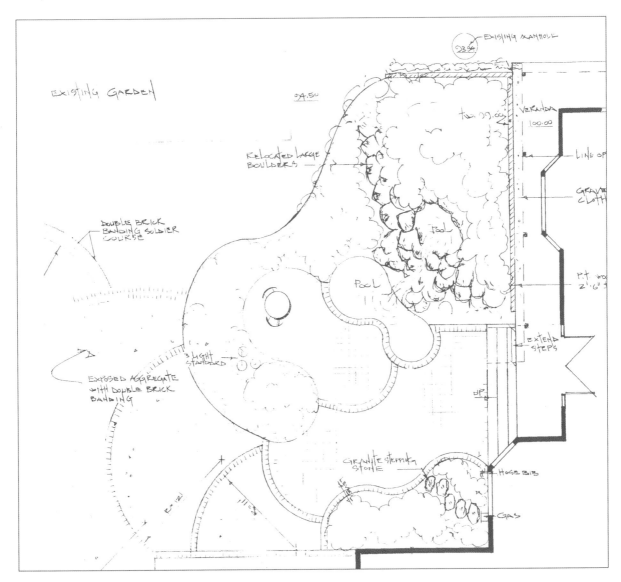

[...and finally...and their hidden room]

[The problem — Arthur and Suzanne had awkward, slippery steps that didn't appear to fit in]

[The solution — Instead of railings, the warmth of brick and two wide, inviting steps that curve for access in all directions]

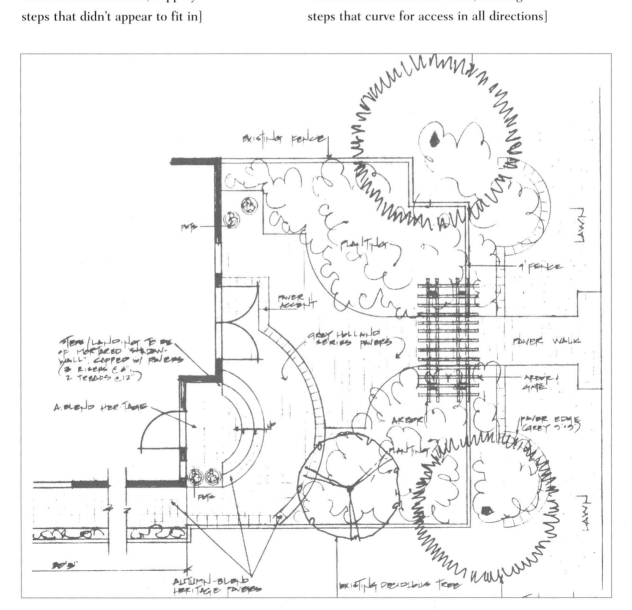

[The two-step solution pictured at top of page]

[Sometimes a wall is just another pretty face]

outdoor den or breakfast nook that captures the view and can be enjoyed when the rest of the garden is in shade?

The romantic porches of days gone by are attractive to the street, and provide protection from the weather, but can darken the house. Skylights can brighten up the porch and the house. Or you can build a porch without a roof, or a separate seating area, at ground level. This room can be part of life on the street, or concealed by a bermed planting bed, or low hedge. No more than 4' high, a bed or hedge like this will not block light or create a security concern.

But the front need not be only an entry. The front may have a view not available anywhere else on the property, and it probably basks in sunlight at different times of the day or year than the back. So why not create an

If you create a proper balance between open and private, you will use and enjoy your front living room and you will be surprised how many of your neighbours will pick up on your ideas.

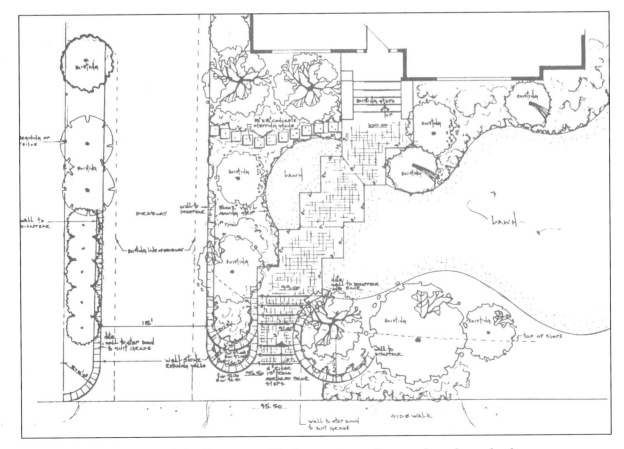

[We widened the driveway and built retaining walls to replace the rocks that cost Sam and Sidney $500 every time they backed their car into them. *See photographs on page 31*]

[Perspective drawing of the new entry — a preview of what's to come]

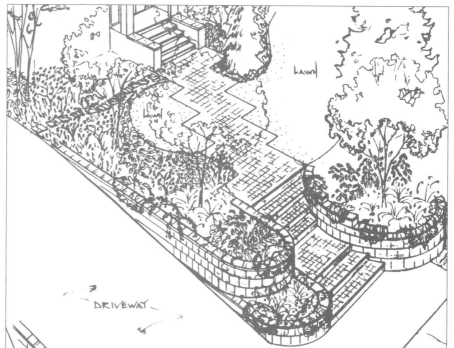

DRIVEWAY

[Before – above left: With no pathway to the house from the street except up the driveway, the house seemed tucked away and inaccessible. This beautiful Tudor-style home deserved better]

[After – above right and left: Curved walls and wide steps bring the front entry out to the street. It's much more inviting when you don't have to look for it]

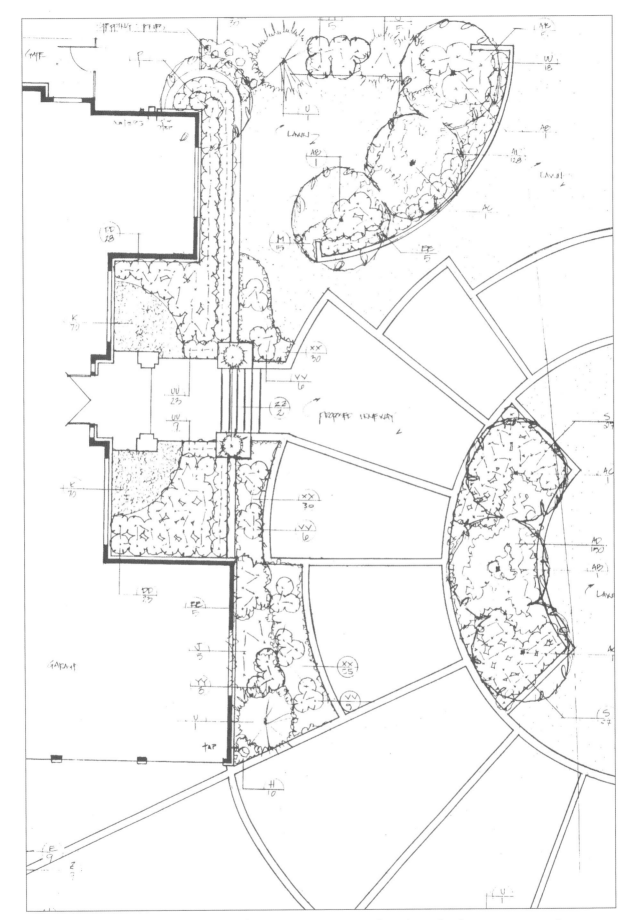

[Driveways can be blended into front entrances. Curve them to make them more attractive, section them to make them more interesting, and wrap them up with colourful plants]

SIDE ROOMS

Side gardens are the skeletons in the closet of landscaping. We seldom discuss them publicly, we take our friends through the house to avoid them, and they never appear in family photos.

But we do pay taxes on them, so why not dress them up so we can take them out?

The challenge is to combine looks and use. As hallways between garden rooms, they should be beautiful. But don't forget to make them a working passage as well. They are intended to be walked on. Pushing a wheelbarrow, lawn mower or bicycle over whatever surface you choose is inevitable. Moss-covered stones may be attractive and romantic, but may also be slippery and uneven. Perhaps concrete or paving stone, at a minimum width of 3'6", would make the journey easier. The path can meander — as long as you don't have to. If you can see the hallway from an inside room, a raised planter would bring the view closer to eye level. Consider arbours and trellises to add a vista and privacy where there was none before. But be careful — remember, an arbour could block light to the inside. Add appropriate plants for the setting, as an artist adds colours in just the right places.

Seems unfinished? A little drab, as hallways often are? Remember that water makes any space come alive. If your side garden is too narrow for a pond, build one at the end of the hallway — visible from the back or front rooms as well. And again — think function: use moving water. It will attract you to the end of the hallway, and it will mask unwanted neighbourhood sounds.

[The green door to the back garden is framed by pink *Cornus Kousa* (Chinese dogwood) trees]

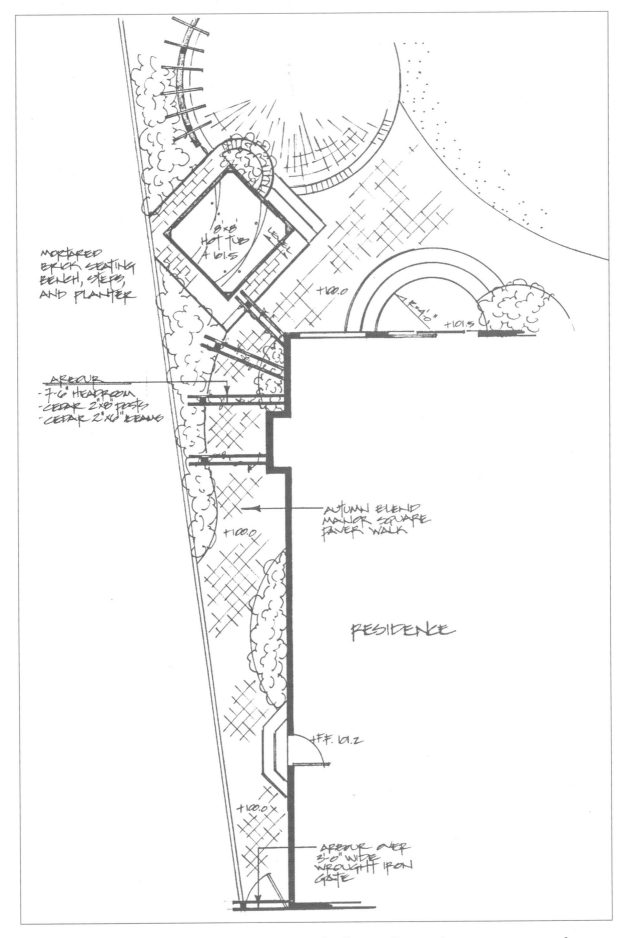

MORTARED
BRICK SEATING
BENCH, STEPS,
AND PLANTER

8'X8'
HOT TUB
@ 101.5

LEVEL
FF

+100.0

+101.5

ARBOUR
- 7'-6" HEADROOM
- CEDAR 2"X8" POSTS
- CEDAR 2"X8" BEAMS

AUTUMN BLEND
MANOR SQUARE
PAVER WALK

+100.0

RESIDENCE

+F.F. 101.2

+100.0

ARBOUR OVER
3'-0" WIDE
WROUGHT IRON
GATE

[Gardening on the side — a design that gives the illusion of space along a narrow passage]

[The problem — A barren, uninviting hallway between the houses had no redeeming features]

Function can become the heart of some side gardens. A hallway is a perfect place to hide a tool shed and storage spaces. Build them like indoor closets — long and narrow with folding doors that allow easy access. They will take up less space and have more usable area inside.

And don't forget the hot tub. It may not be the most attractive feature to look at from inside or out, and you might want to avoid the neighbour's eyes when you are using it. Tuck the hot tub into the side garden. It will still be easily accessible and open up an entirely different view of your garden rooms. That hallway may become your favourite place.

[The solution — Including the entire area (with the neighbour's permission) creates enough space for a clear, wide passageway. Arbour pieces create a sense of moving through a room, and plants soften the harsh, tall wall of the house next door]

A long narrow shed (12'-15' long by 5' outside width) with a sliding or folding door that opens up to 8'-14' for access, depending on the length of the structure, will greatly increase your actual storage space (see drawing below).

If the side garden is just too small to fit a shed into, there are many ways to incorporate a shed into another room, and obscure it or make it an attraction. But that's another book.

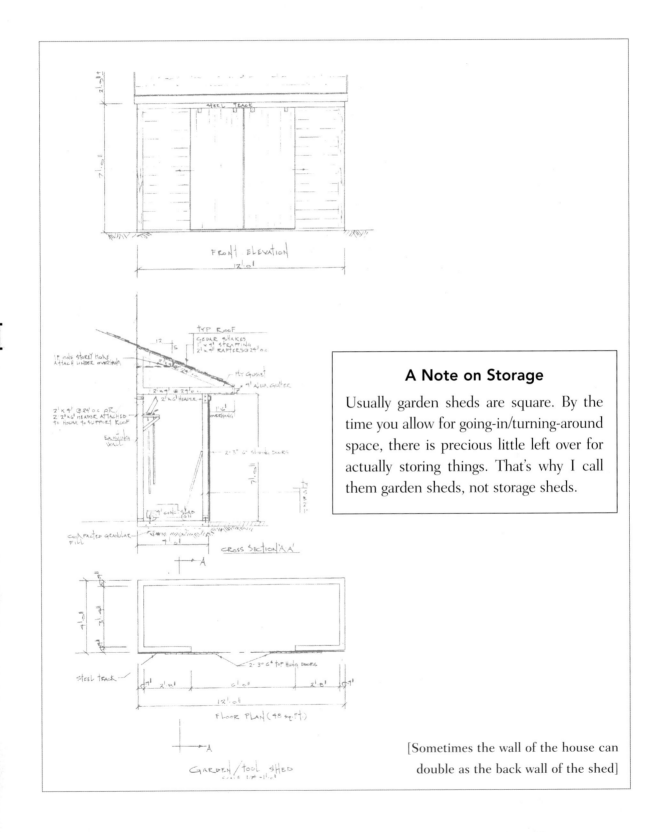

A Note on Storage

Usually garden sheds are square. By the time you allow for going-in/turning-around space, there is precious little left over for actually storing things. That's why I call them garden sheds, not storage sheds.

[Sometimes the wall of the house can double as the back wall of the shed]

BACK ROOMS

By "back rooms" I mean the areas more generally accepted as our outdoor rooms — family rooms, eating nooks, recreation rooms, entertaining rooms. These are the places where we spend most of our outdoor leisure time, and that's fine. There is usually easier access from the house to the back garden. It is sometimes possible to combine forces with your neighbour to create privacy, when it is a mutually desired goal.

Patios, hot tubs, pathways, vegetable gardens, swimming pools, sandboxes, swings, playhouses, arbours, decks, trellises, sheds, water features and anything else you want can be located anywhere you want, with some consideration.

Back to that old sun issue — you can always create shade, but you cannot change the path of the sun. This keeps coming up because it is crucial to the success of your rooms.

Locate the sunniest spot you have as close to the house as possible. That is the most likely area for successful seating, eating, whatever. Make it as big as possible. We use available space. Outdoor rooms do not have to be square. Use any shape you like, as long as hallways are allowed for and curves or corners don't make the space too difficult to use.

[Step in — lie back — sky-gaze]

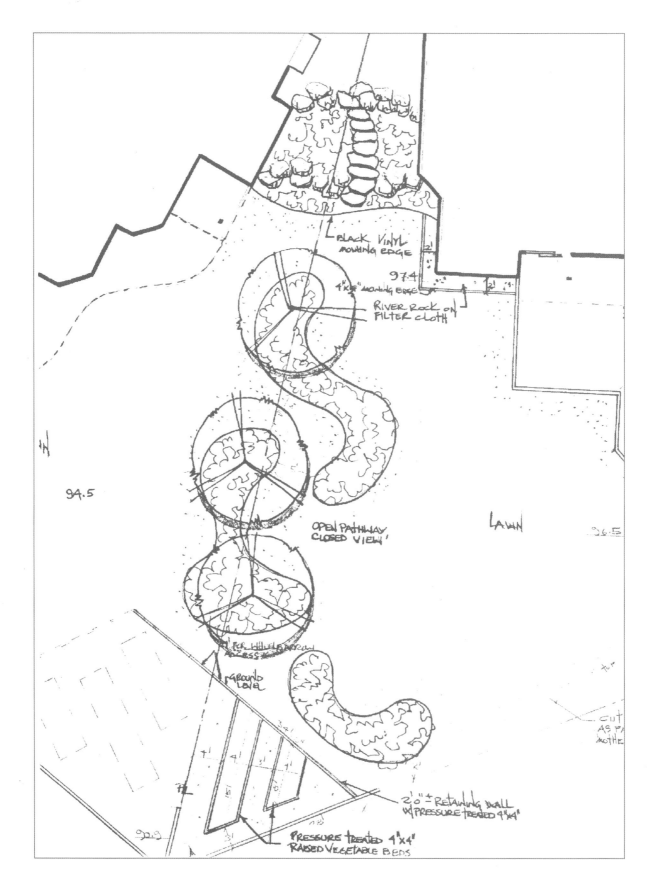

["No fences" make good neighbours too. If you get along with the grumps next door, you can design planting beds that zigzag the property line. Both of you will have a wonderful view, just not of each other, and the lawn wrapping around makes each garden appear bigger than it really is]

Some of your family may prefer sun while others prefer shade. You can have it all in one room, but be cautious: once a room is divided into a sunny spot and a shady spot, it appears smaller. Close to the house, an arbour is probably more suitable than a tree. Just be sure the overhead pieces are close enough together and at the proper angle to block the sun. Even small trees can be heavy and dark in the winter, and they may block your view of other rooms. Work your way out from there.

If the swimming pool is far from the house, or separated from other rooms with a fence, put a large enough seating area around it to be enjoyed while everyone is at the pool.

[Heaven disguised as a hot tub.
See perspective drawing, page 13]

If the storage shed must go in the back, replicate the style and finish of the house, making it attractive and deliberate, or obscure it with plants. Plunking it in the back corner provides very little aesthetic appeal. Make it accessible with a solid path.

Whatever rooms you want, whatever rooms you need, be sure they are created for your enjoyment. They can provide a vacation whenever you need one, without the hassles of lineups, traffic, vaccinations, packing, missing luggage, parking, botched reservations, bad weather and Montezuma's Revenge. Think of creating an island paradise.

[Use your garden like a hardware store. Turn your rocks into lights, or statues or benches — they already fit right in]

[The problem — Frederick and Marion's dull grey, cracked concrete pad, parallel with the edge of the house, made the area seem longer and narrower than it really was]

[The solution — Earth-toned paving stones, a light grey retaining wall and a natural-wood structure over the hot tub create warmth and brightness where before there was none]

[Storage sheds — like the one seen here with the white door — can give privacy to the outdoor family room]

[Warm wooden decks can be built out over unlevelled ground with less work and expense than concrete, paving stones or other surfaces that require retaining walls and backfill]

[The problem — A long, narrow garden surrounded by high walls with planters pointing in one direction made Arthur and Suzanne's yard feel claustrophobic]

[The solution — Curves originating at the centre of the family room add width and create a comfortable place to sit and relax]

[One of the best things about a swimming pool is sitting in the shade
watching others get the exercise that you promised yourself]

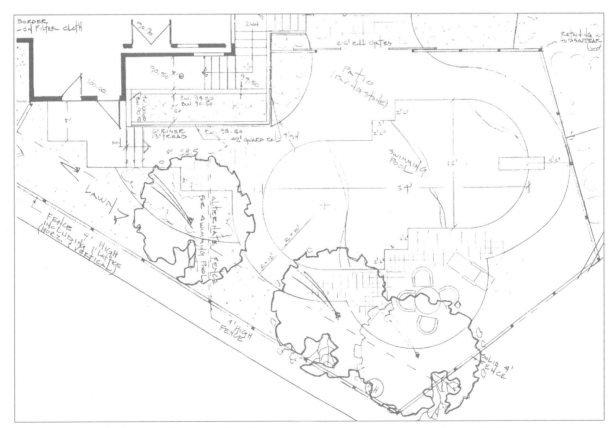

[When you have small children, it makes sense to surround the pool with
lots of patio space and fence it all off from the rest of the garden]

THE GARDEN AS THERAPY

As Mrs. Carlisle explained, gardening has kept her from going crazy. Every weed she pulls has her nasty, noisy neighbour's name on it. "Take that, you old bat, I've had it with you and your chain saw."

Gardening as therapy — physical and mental — is a much discussed, widely accepted theory. But I'm not sure I get it.

What about Shoveller's Arches? Weeder's Knees? Hoer's Elbow? And Planter's Back? What about a well-maintained, well-watered lawn that requires shearing twice a week? What about the luscious hanging baskets and pots demanding water every 20 minutes? And what about the vegetables "lovingly" grown while battling with insects and slugs? What about evenings and weekends given over to such deeds — while we dream of sunny beaches and Monet's garden? This is therapy? The cure that kills? And yet gardeners are the happiest miserable people you will ever meet. They cheerfully complain about the weather — good or bad. They search for weeds under every leaf, optimistically anticipating there will be none. And they blithely shift plants from place to place, looking for the perfect combination.

Yet as we experience construction delays on the road and personal fatigue, we are given the time and tendency to let our minds wander through the garden. Swinging in the hammock, listening to the waterfall, humming with the birds and contemplating the beauty of life are the images we hold fast while commuting, exhaust pipe to exhaust pipe. What are mere aches and pains next to these?

[Richard and Marla's yard is transformed into a breakfast nook and an outdoor entertainment room. Nestled into a berm (a pile of expensive dirt) and surrounded by a pond and waterfall, the stump, barely visible on the far left against the white siding of the tool shed, is now the treasure they always thought it was]

THE NO-MAINTENANCE GARDEN

The no-maintenance garden is as real as the no-maintenance house — it doesn't exist. But good planning can produce a *low*-maintenance garden — or at least one that allows for the amount of time you have to spend, and the type of maintenance you like to do.

Be sure to:

- *Keep a nice flow to lawn edges* and try to avoid tight corners that you will have to mow. Having to get out the clippers or weed eater adds time and frustration to the task.

- *Add a mowing edge.* This is anything that divides the lawn from something else — a planting bed, a retaining wall, a fence, etc. It can be pressure-treated wood, mortared brick or black plastic. Ideally you can run the wheel of the lawn mower over it.

- *Put the right plant in the right place.* The spacing should allow for the plant's mature size, or in the case of a hedge, the size you will maintain it at. Include enough plants so that they will grow together within two or three years and cover the ground. The

[You can keep your lawn edge crisp and clean with a brick mowing edge cemented in place]

[Beware: Falling asleep at night, you'll be able to hear the lawn growing over the stepping stones. Keep your nail clippers handy]

amount of weeding will then be minimal. It's the right plant if the soil and light conditions it will get are the ones it wants. It's the right plant if it's the right size for that spot, and you don't have to keep hacking it into an unrecognizable shape to keep it there. It's the right plant if it doesn't grow taller than the ones in the bed behind it. And it's the right plant if you like it. If not, choose another one.

- *Use a mulch of well-composted bark* (2") in newly planted beds to add goodness to the soil, and help keep the weeds down while the plants fill in their allotted space.

- *Increase hard surfaces.* As mentioned before, installed properly, they will require less maintenance over the long term. Use rock, concrete pavers, pressure-treated wood, mortared brick, aluminum railings, etc., that have a long shelf life.

- *Plant trees in beds, not lawn.* The water required to create lush, green lawns far exceeds the amount required by trees. Excess water at the trunks of trees can encourage fungi that can damage or kill them. On the other hand, there are trees that thrive in such conditions, and trees interrupting expanses of rolling green grass conjure up romantic images of blankets and picnics. So think about whether you have the extra time and energy needed to cut around trees, and if your garden is big enough to achieve the desired effect.

- *Weed every day.* Take ten minutes getting from the car to the house after work or while you go to dump the compost. Stir up the surface of the planting beds to discourage new weeds from rooting and uproot the stubborn survivors of previous battles. It might relieve some of the day's stresses, and it's amazing how much time this will free up on the weekends when you have so many other things to do.

- *Borrow a landscape.* I don't mean after midnight when no one is looking. Frame, with plantings or with windows in walls, your neighbour's beautiful tree or a distant mountain view. There is no additional work required, and your garden seems much larger because of it.

- *Invite company for a barbecue.* This is one of my biggest incentives to get the garden cleaned up.

PLANT LIST
Plan # 10   May 1997

EXP. (Exposure):
S - Sun
Sh - Shade
PSh - Part Shade

TYPE:
B - Biennial
C - Coniferous
D - Deciduous
E - Evergreen
G - Ground Cover
Gr - Grass
P - Perennial
S - Shrub
T - Tree
V - Vine

KEY	BOTANICAL NAME	QTY	SIZE	SPACING	TYPE	EXP.	COMMON NAME / REMARKS
A	Acer palmatum 'Sango Kaku'	1	5' ht.	per plan	DT	S, Sh	Coral Bark Maple/cream-grn leaves, pink bark
B	Campanula x 'Birch Hybrid'	38	1 gal.	12-18" oc	P	S, PSh	Bellflower/purple-blue bell, flws summer, trailing form
C	Eupatorium purpureum 'Atropurpurea'	3	1 gal.	3'0" oc	P	S, PSh	Joe-Pye Weed, purple umbrella flw clusters – summer/fall
D	Geranium x 'Johnson Blue'	36	1 gal.	18-24" oc	P	S, PSh	Blue Cranesbill/large loose blue flws - summer, mound of lvs
E	Heather (fall)	7	1 gal.	18" oc	ES	S, PSh	Calluna vulgaris/spikes of tiny bell flws – fall
F	Heather (winter)	7	1 gal.	18" oc	ES	S, PSh	Erica carnea/small bell-like flws – winter
G	Helleborus niger	13	1 gal.	18-24" oc	P	PSh, Sh	Christmas Rose/large white-grn rose-like flws – Nov/Dec
H	Hosta sieboldiana 'Elegans'	3	1 gal.	2'0" oc	P	Sh, PSh	Plantain Lily/fleshy large blue-green lvs, lilac flw – summer
I	Hydrangea serrata 'Bluebird'	5	5 gal.	3'0"	DS	S, Sh	Lacecap Hydrangea/blue domed flw clusters in summer
J	Iberis sempervirens	5	1 gal.	12-18" oc	EG, P	S	Candytuft/flat white flw clusters – Apr, trailing, low
K	Iris pallida 'Aureo-variegata'	35	1 gal.	18" oc	P	SD, PSh	Sweet Iris/lav-blue flws, summer, variegated grassy lvs
L	Kalmia latifolia 'Elf'	5	2 gal.	2'0" oc	ES	PSh, S	Dwarf Mt. Laurel/spring saucer pink flws, red buds, glossy lvs
M	Liatris spicata 'Kobold'	6	1 gal.	18" oc	P	S	Gay Feather/mauve flw spikes – summer, compact plant
N	Raphiolepis indica rosea 'Harbinger of Spring'	5	5 gal.	30" oc	ES	S	Indian Hawthorn/loose, pink summer flws, new foliage red
O	Rhododendron 'Impeditum'	14	1 gal.	2'0" oc	ES	S, PSh	Purple-blue flowers in early April, low size
P	Rhododendron 'P.J.M.'	6	5 gal.	3'0" oc	ES	S, PSh	Bright lavender-pink flws, early February, medium size
Q	Sarcococca hookeriana humilis	25	1 gal.	2'0" oc	ES	Sh, PSh	Himalayan Sweet Box/white fragrant flws – April, glossy lvs
R	Viburnum plicatum tomentosum 'Mariesii'	1	5 gal.	5'0"	DS	S, PSh	Marie's Dble. File Viburnum/flat spring white flw clusters
S	Blechnum spicant	23	1 gal.	18" oc	ES	S, PSh	Deer Fern/glossy dark green tufted fronds
T	Hydrangea anomala	2	2 gal.		DV	S, PSh	Climbing Hydrangea/flat white flw clusters – June, glossy lvs
U	Pachysandra terminalis variegata	35	4" pot	12" oc	EG	Sh	Japanese Spurge/white flw spikes – spring, grn/white lvs

Note: The designation "oc" in the spacing column refers to "on centre" and is the distance from the centre of one plant to the centre of the next plant in its grouping.

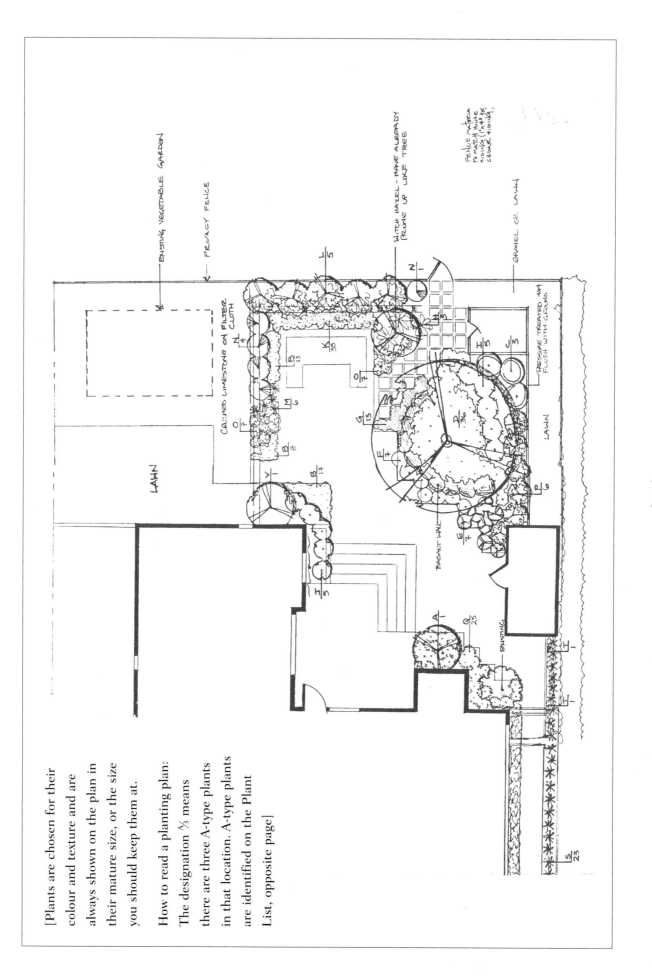

[Plants are chosen for their colour and texture and are always shown on the plan in their mature size, or the size you should keep them at.

How to read a planting plan: The designation $A/3$ means there are three A-type plants in that location. A-type plants are identified on the Plant List, opposite page]

ENSTING VEGETABLE GARDEN

PRIVACY FENCE

WITCH HAZEL – HAVE ALREADY PRUNE UP LIKE TREE

FENCE MATERIAL TO MATCH HOUSE SIDING (1 x 4 & 1 x 6 CEDAR SIDING)

GRAVEL OR LAWN

CRUSHED LIMESTONE ON FILTER CLOTH

PRESSURE TREATED 4 x 4 FLUSH WITH GROUND

LAWN

BASALT WALL

ENSTING

LAWN

THE PERFECT PLANTS

All plants are perfect — in the right place. The biggest difficulty is struggling through the maze of possibilities.

Be aware of the type of home you have to offer your new plants. You don't have to know exactly which plant you want, but you do need to know how big or wide you want it to be, how much light it will get, if it will be wet or dry and the type of soil it will have to live in.

If it can do its own thing in its new home, and you only have to prune out the inevitable dead parts, you have made a wise choice.

In general, I believe most coniferous trees are too big for residential gardens. Although they are beautiful, graceful and elegant, they take whatever room they need, often to the detriment of your living space or other plants. Consider carefully before you plant them. The same with a lot of deciduous trees. Visit botanical gardens. The plants are labelled. You will know if you have the same setting for them to grow in. You can see their mature size. You will make better decisions.

[Hanging baskets can be a nuisance to care for, but they sure dress up a hallway]

[Outdoor rooms will also be enjoyed from indoor rooms, if you design them that way]

Plan for colour. When the first warm rays of spring sunshine beam down on us, we race to the nursery and purchase everything that's blooming. And why not? It has been months since such colour and scents brought us hope. They inspire us to "garden on." No bed of weeds is too big to tackle and no lawn too tedious to cut. Mother Nature is once again our friend.

Then spring ends and summer brings lazy days to lounge in our garden rooms. Where have all the flowers gone? The problem is that most of us plant spring-flowering gardens. By early summer everything is only green again — except the hanging baskets. And if we get tired of replacing them every year, and watering them twice a day, we will have no flowers at all.

With a little bit of effort, we can avoid this boom-and-bust cycle and have exciting gardens year-round. Try combining the unique branching patterns of some deciduous plants in winter, the variety of shrubs and perennials that bloom in different seasons, grasses that remain statuesque all winter, and the many textures and colours of coniferous and broad-leaved evergreen plants. You will have a garden that delights all year.

It's the thought, the planning before the planting, that counts.

[Jennifer and Geoff's original pond]

THE MAGIC OF WATER

Once upon a time, the design I unrolled for Jennifer and Geoff included a small raised wooden pond with a spill rock at the back.

"What's that?" comes the immediate question, Geoff's finger pointing at the pond.

"It's a small water feature," I beam.

"I don't want a water feature," is his reply.

"You might," I persist.

"Definitely not," is his reply.

"Maybe you could think about it for a while before you decide," I persist.

"Don't need to; I don't want it."

Now the customer is always right — except when his wife is standing behind him, making all kinds of gestures indicating that she wants the pond, and it's up to me to get it. I know now that someone is going to end up unhappy.

[Their latest, greatest version]

"I am so convinced that you'll love it, that while completing the rest of the garden, we'll put in the pond, and if you don't absolutely love it, we'll take it out." If only these types of thoughts would linger a few moments in my mind instead of immediately jumping out of my mouth. He agrees. The customer is also always smart. They loved it. Yellow rubber ducks were given a home. I had done the right thing.

A year or so later Geoff called.

"Remember you said you would take the pond out if we didn't like it?"

We? I think. "Yes," I reply. The world stops turning and my stomach starts.

"Well, we don't like it. We want a bigger one."

Never underestimate the magic of water.

[Ponds are like children...]

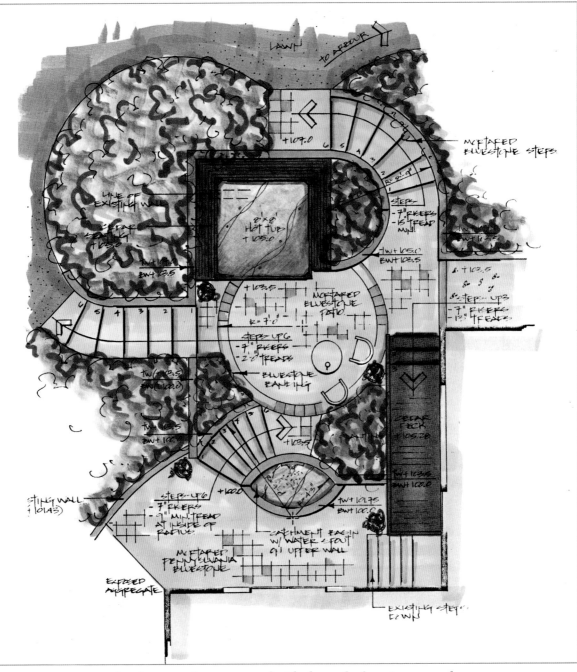

[...the more time you spend with them, the happier you are]

Water is the magic that can turn a boring corner of your yard into the place where people gather. Water hides unpleasant sounds. It adds a beautiful sound of its own. Add fish and plants, and you have something to watch, not just look at.

The question, then, is not "if," but "where?" Maximize your investment by choosing a place where you can see it from the most windows in your home. It is something to be enjoyed, so don't hide it. Proximity to the house may also cut down on predators. Add lights for nighttime viewing.

Ponds at, or near, the front entry set a peaceful, quiet mood that visitors carry into the house.

[Water — you can walk right up and touch it...]

[...invite friends to fish-watch...]

[...or spend quiet time beside it together — alone]

[Build your pond conveniently close to where you live — indoors and outdoors...]

Ponds in the back yard offer a surprise after people step out. A pond is a magnet for pleasant conversation — and compliments. It can be the central point of your garden, or the framework for a distant view. It can be rapidly flowing or peaceful and calm — or a combination of the two, depending on your mood.

Avoid locating your pond too close to large trees — the shade may be too heavy. Also, excavation may be difficult because of the roots, and needles or leaves that fall may pollute the water and add to maintenance.

[...grow up with it — ponds are magnets for kids from 1 to 92...]

[...frame it — make the view from inside like a picture on your wall]

[A quick recipe for transforming mess into magic...]

[...just add water to the pile of dirt and rock — "eau de lightful"]

Use the shape of your home and garden to help you decide how the pond should be designed, but don't be dictated to. Let your desire be your final guide. The style and choice of construction materials is wide-ranging. Concrete, pond liner, preformed liners, half barrels, drilled rocks and other materials give you an endless choice. It is like painting with many colours. The results are limited only by your imagination.

No area is too small, too barren, or too lost to be brought to life with water. Imagine sitting by the cooling spray, watching the birds and dragonflies, and listening to the frogs.

Think big. No one has ever complained that their pond should have been smaller.

[Surround sound...]

[...or absolute quiet — both are music to the ears]

[Even a thimble-sized pond (2' across) can fill your heart]

P.S.

One last small note: Big projects can dramatically alter your garden and possibly your outlook on life. But you can still look like a brilliant designer with just the smallest strokes of imagination.

Look at that bed of flowers. Now put a spade in the ground and make the bed a bit wider and presto, you have painted an image like an artist. Or how about that pathway? Suppose you put a curve in it and redirect it? Then you have a whole new way of entering your world.

Digging a pond can do the same, as can enlarging a patio or creating shade or privacy where you currently don't have it. What you give yourself is something new that came from you. And all these require the same process and dedication as mega-projects.

But don't forget to consider the entire garden when you do anything, because whatever you do has to fit into the overall area. Be thoughtful. Be daring. But pay attention to details and don't put big shrubs in front of little flowers.

And take pictures! Those "before and after" photos will make for "wows" and congratulations for years to come.

57

ORDER FORM

Landscaping Made Easy By Design ~ **by Ruth Olde**

Also available at your local bookstore.

__ copies at $22.95 = $ _____	__ copies at US$19.95 = $ _____
+ G.S.T. at 7% = $ _____	
B.C. residents add:	
P.S.T. at 7% = $ _____	
Shipping & handling:	**Shipping & handling:**
First copy: $6.95 = $ _____	First copy: US$5.50 = $ _____
Additional: $3.00 ea. = $ _____	Additional: US$2.00 ea. = $ _____
Total enclosed = $ _____	**Total enclosed = US$** _____

Name: ....

Street Address: ....

City or Town: ....

Province or State: ....

Postal or Zip Code: ....

Home Phone: ....

Business Phone: ....

E-mail: ....

Please make cheques and money orders payable to:
Blasig Landscape Design & Construction Ltd.

Please send completed order form with payment to:
**Box 342, Maple Ridge, B.C.
Canada V2X 7G2**

Enquiries:
Telephone: **(604) 462-9144**
or visit our web site: **www.blasig.com**

Thank you for your order!